JAPANESE

Colophon

© 2002 Rebo International b.v., Lisse, The Netherlands

www.rebo-publishers.com - info@rebo-publishers.com

This 2nd edition reprinted 2004

Original recipes and photographs: © R&R Publishing Pty. Ltd.

Design, editing, production and typesetting: Minkowsky Graphics, Enkhuizen, The Netherlands

ISBN 90 366 1473 2

JAPANESE

the sophistication of miso siru
and sukiyaki is the very height of

creative cooking

REBO
PUBLISHERS

Foreword

Japan is an island empire. The surrounding seas are heated by Kuroshio, the plankton-rich Japanese Stream, which is full of fish, crustaceans and shellfish. The islands themselves are mountainous and the small amount of agricultural land is terraced, flooded, and planted with rice and other crops. The Japanese population has always lived on the harvest from the sea and from the paddyfields. The cuisine is a reflection of what the nature offers.

Japanese cuisine is typified by its masterly simplicity and sublime refinement. The preparation of the food involves contemplation and meditation. If you take infinite pains with the preparation of these recipes, then your cooking will become an art.

More culinary Japan

If you fall under the spell of Japanese cuisine

through trying the recipes

in this book that you long for more recipes,

we would like to draw

your attention to the book

SUSHI & SASHIMI that is available

in the same series.

Method

Heat the chicken and beef broths in a saucepan and add the shiitake mushrooms and sliced ginger. Bring the broths to the boil then simmer for 5 minutes. Remove from the heat and allow to rest for 40 minutes.

Remove the mushrooms from the liquid and carefully slice them, discarding stems. Remove the ginger from the broth and set aside. Line a sieve with some paper towel then pour the broth into the sieve. Allow the broth to drain through the sieve, straining out all the grit and sand from the mushrooms. Discard the paper.

Return the strained broth, ginger, and shittake mushrooms to the saucepan and bring to a simmer. Add the sesame oil, five-spice powder, teriyaki sauce, mirin, and finely sliced mushrooms and simmer for 10 minutes.

Remove the ginger and add the sliced green (spring) onions.

Serve the soup in Japanese bowls, garnished with the sesame seeds.

*Available from Asian food stores.

Ingredients

4 cups/1¾ pints/1 l chicken broth

2 cups/16fl oz/500ml beef broth

50g/2oz dried shiitake mushrooms

1oz/30g piece fresh ginger, sliced

1 tsp/5g toasted sesame oil

1 tsp/5g five-spice powder

Green Onion, Sesame, and Shiitake Soup

1 tbsp/15ml teriyaki sauce*

2 tbsp/30ml mirin*

⅔ cup/3½ oz/100g button mushrooms, finely sliced

6 green (spring) onions, sliced diagonally

1 tbsp/15g sesame seeds

Japanese

Method

1. Cook shrimp in boiling water for 1 minute, remove, and place in iced water immediately. Slice in half lengthwise.

2. Place nori sheet, shiny side down, on a bamboo mat (makisu). Spread it with ½ cup/4oz/125g of rice, leaving a 1cm space at top and bottom of seaweed. Place half the shrimp, lettuce, cucumber, avocado, flying-fish roe, and mayonnaise across the middle of the rice.

3. Carefully roll up the nori, using the bamboo mat. Roll tightly to ensure the filling is held in place. Remove bamboo mat.

4. Using a wet, sharp knife, cut roll into 8 even sized pieces.

California Rolls (California Maki)

Ingredients

4 green shrimp, peeled and deveined

2 sheets nori seaweed

1 cup/8oz/250g prepared sushi rice (su-meshi)

½ cup/2oz/50g shredded lettuce

1 small cucumber, cut into strips lengthwise

½ avocado, sliced

1 tbsp/15g flying fish roe

1½ tbsp/45ml mayonnaise

Method

1. Cook udon noodles in boiling water for 8 minutes, until tender.

2. Pour hot udonji into a serving bowl. Spoon in hot cooked udon noodles.

3. Overlap slices of beef onto the noodles, covering half the bowl. Add green onions and tempura batter pieces to the soup.

4. Sprinkle sesame seeds over the soup and serve.

Beef Udon Noodle Soup (Niku Udon)

Ingredients

3oz/80g udon noodles

1 cup/8fl oz/250ml udonji, heated

2oz/50g beef tenderloin, sliced very thinly

1 tbsp/15g sliced green (spring) onions

1 tbsp/15g cooked tempura batter pieces

½ tsp/2.5g ground white sesame seeds

Japanese

Method

1. Simmer kelp in rice vinegar for 5–10 minutes, or until soft.

2. Wet a wooden sushi mold or line a rectangular container measuring 10inx3inx2in/25cmx7.5cmx6cm with cling film. Allow the cling film to overhang by at least 4in/10cm oneach side.

3. Arrange one-third of the salmon over the mold to cover. Sprinkle with one-third of the shiso leaves. Spoon over 1 ½ cups/12oz/350g rice, gently press down. Repeat with another third of salmon, a third of shiso, then the remaining rice, remaining salmon, and shiso. Top with strips of cooked kelp.

4. Place the wet wooden lid on the mold, or cover with overhanging plastic wrap. Place a weight on top and leave for at least four hours, or overnight.

5. Carefully remove the compressed sushi from the mold or container and unwrap. Using a wet, sharp knife, cut into eight equal portions and serve.

Ingredients

1 kelp sheet

Around ½ cup/4fl oz/125ml rice vinegar

4oz/120g salmon, cut into slices ¼in/5mm thick

5 shiso leaves, cut into ¼in/5mm strips

3 cups/1lb 10oz/750g prepared sushi rice

Salmon Box Sushi (Sake Hako Sushi)

Japanese

Method

1. Arrange sliced fish decoratively on a large serving platter. Place sliced abalone into cleaned shell.

2. Combine silver bream, green onion, and ginger, and stir well. Spoon onto platter.

3. Garnish liberally with lemon, lime, dill, cucumber, and seaweed. Serve with wasabi paste.

Ingredients

5 thin, bite-sized slices each of tuna, salmon, garfish, snapper, grouper, or other suitable white fish

1¼lb/500g abalone, removed from shell, cleaned and sliced

2½oz/60g silver bream, cut into ¼in/5mm strips

1 green (spring) onion, minced

½ tsp/2.5g chopped picked ginger

Assorted Sashimi (Sashimi Moriawase)

To decorate:

sliced lemon and lime, sprigs of dill,

sliced cucumber, seaweed, etc.

Method

1. Place mackerel fillet skin-side down in a flat dish. Cover liberally with salt. Leave for one hour.

2. Remove mackerel, shake off excess salt. Return to an empty flat dish and cover with rice vinegar. Allow to marinate for one hour. Remove and wipe dry with kitchen paper.

3. Place kelp in saucepan, cover with rice vinegar, and simmer for 5 minutes. Remove and drain.

4. Place kelp onto a bamboo mat (makisu). Arrange mountain pepper leaves evenly down the center, place mackerel, skin-side down over the kelp. Spoon rice on top, and press down with wet fingers. Ensure that the rice is of even thickness and flat along its surface. Gently roll the sushi with the bamboo mat to create a rounded top to the mackerel. Remove and sit the sushi upright on its rice base. Cut into six even pieces with a wet sharp knife.

Mackerel Bou Sushi (Saba Bou Sushi)

Ingredients

1 mackerel fillet, all small bones removed

salt

rice vinegar

2inx4in/5cmx10cm kelp sheet

6 Japanese mountain pepper leaves

2 cups/1 lb/500g prepared sushi rice

Japanese

Method

1. Cut fish into pieces measuring approximately 1in/2.5cm wide by 2in/5cm long.

2. Cook shrimp in boiling water for one minute, remove and place in iced water immediately. Gently cut along underside of shrimp, though not all the way through, and open out flat.

3. Wet your hand and pick up a 1 tbsp /¾oz–1oz/20g–25g portion of rice. Gently shape the rice into a rectangle, wetting the hands as often as necessary. The rice portion should be slightly smaller than the topping.

4. Using your finger spread a little wasabi on the underside of each piece of fish. Place the seafood on top and gently press together. Repeat with desired amount of ingredients. Serve with pickled ginger (gari) and shoyu (Japanese soy sauce).

Ingredients

assorted sliced fish (approximately ⅛in/3mm thick) e.g. tuna, salmon, grouper, scrod, shad or other very fresh white fish

shrimp, peeled and deveined

prepared sushi rice (su-meshi)

wasabi paste

Assorted Sushi (Sushi Moriawase)
Shaped Sushi (Nigiri-Zushi)

Method

1. Slice scallops almost in half, through the center. Open out to create an oval shape, press lightly to flatten.

2. Heat a griddle and oil lightly. Sear scallops, salmon, and swordfish on one side for three seconds only. Remove carefully from griddle.

3. Wet your hands and take 1 tbsp/20g–25g portion of rice. Gently shape the rice into a rectangule, wetting hands as often as necessary. The rice portion should be slightly smaller than the topping.

4. Using your finger, spread a little wasabi on the underside of the seafood. Place a piece of seafood on top, broiled side up. Gently press together. Repeat with remaining ingredients.

Ingredients

2 medium scallops, without orange roe removed

2 very thinly slices salmon (approximately 1inx3in/3cmx7cm)

2 thin slices swordfish (approximately 1inx3in/3cmx7cm)

1 cup/8oz/250g prepared sushi rice

wasabi

Lightly Seared Sushi (Aburi Sushi)

Note:

for a more decorative pattern, cook

fish on a heated cake rack, place over

a grill or under a broiler.

Method

1. Cook shrimp in boiling water for one minute. Place into iced water to cool immediately. Carefully cut along underside of shrimp, though not all the way through and open out flat.

2. Cut a shallow cross into the top of each shiitake mushroom and cook in boiling water for one minute. Remove and drain.

3. Lay out two pieces of fish, slightly overlapping on an 8inx8in/20cmx20cm piece of plastic wrap. Place a ball of sushi rice, about the size of a golf ball on top. Bring the corners of the plastic wrap together over the rice, twist, and squeeze until the rice forms a perfect ball. Remove plastic and place sushi ball on a flat serving platter, rice side downward. Repeat process with remaining fish, butterflied shrimp, mushrooms, cucumber, and egg.

4. Top the salmon sushi ball with a little caviar. Decorate the snapper with Japanese mountain pepper leaves, and place some grated daikon and chili pepper on the mushrooms. Spoon some salmon roe over the boiled egg and top the sardines with grated ginger and chopped green onion. Serve with pickled ginger.

Ingredients

3 green shrimp, shelled and deveined

3 shiitake mushrooms

6 thin salmon slices (2inx1in/5cmx2.5cm each)

6 thin tuna slices (2inx1in/5cmx2.5cm each)

6 slices baby snapper (2inx1in/5cmx2.5cm each)

½ cucumber, sliced
into thin 2inx1in/5cmx2.5cm pieces

1 hard-boiled egg, chopped

3 vinegar-cured sardine fillets

1 cup/8oz/250g sushi rice

Assorted Sushi Balls (Temari Sushi)

Toppings:

caviar, grated daikon and chili pepper,

Japanese mountain pepper leaves, salmon roe,

grated ginger, and minced green (spring)

onion, pickled ginger

Japanese

Method

1. Place a sheet of seaweed on a bamboo mat (makisu). Spoon ½ cup/4oz/125g rice onto seaweed. Using wet fingers press rice out evenly, right to the edges.

2. Place a sheet of plastic wrap on top of rice and carefully turn mat over so that the rice is now on the bottom. Remove bamboo mat.

3. Arrange one of the fillings along the center of the seaweed. Using the mat, roll up.

4. Carefully remove the plastic wrap. Sprinkle with the topping and cut with a wet sharp knife into eight equal portions. Repeat with other toppings. Serve with pickled ginger.

Ingredients

Fillings: sliced eel, sliced cucumber, blanched shrimp, topped with finely chopped hard- boiled egg.

Tuna strips, salmon strips, sliced cucumber, chilli, mayonnaise, sliced avocado, topped with white sesame seeds.

Calamari strips, plum paste, sliced cucumber, sliced daikon, topped with tobiko.

Sun-dried tomato, crumbled feta cheese, sliced cucumber, topped with minced green (spring) onion.

Inside-Out Roll (Ura Maki)

Japanese

4 sheets nori seaweed

2 cups/1lb/500g prepared sushi rice

pickled ginger

Method

1. Cut calamari into three equal pieces for three different dishes.

2. For the calamari roll, make shallow outlines 2in/5mm apart on the outside of one calamari piece. Turn calamari over, cut side down. Cut seaweed to the shape of the calamari and place on top. Line up cucumber along centre and roll up. Slice into rolls around ½in/1cm thick. Serve with wasabi and soy sauce.

3. Cut next piece of calamari into ¼in/5mm thick strips. Arrange calamari in a martini glass and spoon over udonji. Garnish with chives.

4. Finally, cut last piece of calamari into ¼in/5mm thick strips and mix with plum paste. Serve in a shallow dish sprinkled with white sesame seeds.

Assorted Calamari Sashimi (Ika Moriawase)

Ingredients

1 large cleaned calamari tube

1 sheet nori seaweed

2 strips cucumber

wasabi paste

soy sauce

2 tbsp udonji

chives

1 tsp plum paste

white sesame seeds

Method:

1. Place noodles and spinach in a heatproof serving bowl. Pour custard into the bowl, cover and steam for 10 minutes.

2. Meanwhile pour udonji into a sauce pan, bring to the boil and add snow peas and crab meat. Cook for 2–3 minutes.

3. Mix arrowroot with one tbsp water and add to the udonji. Stir until it has thickened. Pour liquid over custard and garnish custard with the crab claw and leek.

Ingredients

2oz/60g udon noodles, cooked

3 spinach leaves, steamed

⅓ cup/3½oz/100ml Japanese custard mix

⅓ cup3½ fl oz/100ml udonji

Steamed Japanese Custard with Udon Noodles and Crab (Kani Odamushi)

5 small snow peas

1½oz/40g steamed crabmeat

2 tsp/10g arrowroot

1 steamed crab claw

1 tbsp/15g julienned leek

Method

1. Soak seaweed in water for 5 minutes, and drain.

2. Place fish broth, miso, and ginger in a large saucepan. Bring to the boil.

3. Clean lobster head, separate the legs and claws. Add to the fish broth. When broth returns to the boil, remove the lobster.

4. Heat the miso soup and pour into a large serving bowl. Put hot lobster into the bowl. Arrange seaweed around lobster. Decorate with chives and serve.

Lobster Miso Soup (Ise Ebi Miso Siru)

Ingredients

3 tbsp/45g mixed dried seaweed eg.

ogonori, wakame, tosakanori

4 cups/1¾ pints/ 1l fish broth

2 tsp/70g miso

½ tsp/2.5g grated ginger

1 lobster, head section and legs only

7fl oz/200ml miso soup

Method

1. Carefully break the shell away from the thick end of each crab leg. Leave the thin end of the leg still covered with shell.

2. Make the tempura batter. Dust the crabmeat lightly with flour. Dip the meat end of the crab stick into the tempura batter. Deep fry the whole leg at 360°F/180°C until the batter is crisp and golden.

3. Gently tie each of the seaweed strips into a knot, dip into the tempura batter and deep fry until crispy.

4. Arrange the crab on a large serving plate and garnish with lemon wedges and fried seaweed.

5. See page 40 for tempura batter recipe.

Ingredients

6 large crab legs

plain flour

1 scant cup/7fl oz/200ml tempura batter

1 sheet nori seaweed, cut into 2in/5cm strips

lemon wedges

Tempura Crab (Kani Tenpura)

Method

1. Remove tail from lobster. Cut along underside of shell and remove tail flesh. Remove intestinal tract.

2. Thoroughly wash lobster flesh in water chilled with ice cubes for 5–10 seconds. Dry with paper towel. Cut into small bite-size pieces.

3. Arrange lobster shell on a large flat platter. Spoon the flesh into the upturned tail shell. Serve with wasabi paste and sushi soy sauce.

4. Garnish platter with shiso leaves, cucumber, and sliced daikon.

Lobster Sashimi (Ise Ebi Otsukuri)

Ingredients

1 whole lobster (1 lb 12oz/800g)

wasabi paste

sushi soy sauce

To garnish: shiso leaves

cucumber, daikon

Method

1. Remove legs and tail shell from the shrimp. Devein the shrimp neatly.

2. Carefully lift up the shell covering the head of the shrimp, leaving it still partially attached at the tip.

3. Make cutlines along the stomach of the shrimp, about 8–10 cuts horizontally. Only cut halfway into the stomach. Turn over and squeeze the back of the shrimp so it becomes straight.

4. Dust shrimp lightly with flour and dip into the tempura batter. Deep fry at 360°F/180°C until crisp and golden.

5. Dip nori squares into tempura batter and deep fry until crispy. Serve shrimp on a flat platter, piled on top of each other. Garnish with nori.

Ingredients

3 jumbo shrimp

all-purpose flour

1 scant cup/7fl oz/200ml tempura batter

1 sheet nori seaweed, cut into 4 squares

Tempura Jumbo Shrimp (Ebi Tenpura)

Method

1. Arrange oysters on a bed of crushed ice.

2. Spoon ponzu soy sauce over two oysters and top with a little grated daikon and momizi oroshi, to taste.

3. Spoon undonji over another two oysters and put a pinch of yuzu peel on each and a little salmon roe (ikura).

4. Spoon tosazu dressing over the last two oysters and top with a mixture of finely diced tomato, zucchini, and daikon.

Assorted Topped Oysters (Namagaki)

Ingredients

6 oysters

2 tbsp/30ml ponzu soy sauce

grated daikon

moniji oroshi (chilli paste)

2 tbsp/30ml udonji

yuzu peel

salmon roe (ikura)

1 tbsp/15ml tosazu dressing

finely diced tomato

finely diced zucchini

finely diced daikon

Method

1. Combine all marinade ingredients in a saucepan. Stir over medium heat until salt and sugar have dissolved. Remove from heat and cool. Place salmon in a bowl, cover with the marinade and allow to marinate for 8 hours.

2. Remove salmon, wipe dry with a paper towel. Brush with a little olive oil and cut into very thin slices.

3. Arrange salmon on serving plate, overlapping slices slightly. Blend shiso pistou ingredients to form a smooth sauce. Spoon over salmon.

4. Sprinkle with the green onions and serve.

Orange Marinated Salmon with Shiso Pistou (Sake Orange Tsuke Shiso Huumi)

Ingredients

orange marinade:

4 cups/1¾ pints/1 litre water, juice of 1 orange

juice of 1 lemon, 1 cup/250g/8oz coarse salt

¼ cup/2oz/50g sugar, 3 bay leaves

1 tsp/5g Chinese five-spice

12 mint leaves, 7oz/200g salmon fillet

shiso pistou:

5 shiso leaves

2 tsp/10ml olive oil

1 tbsp/15g minced onion

½ tsp mustard

2 tbsp/30g minced green (spring) onion, green part only

Method

1. Cook soba noodles in boiling water for 5-6 minutes, until tender. Drain well.

2. Divide noodles into 4, and shape each into a small ball. Deep fry each ball carefully until golden brown. Take care while frying to retain the shape of each ball. Drain on kitchen paper.

3. Toss each slice of duck breast lightly in arrowroot. Bring a pan of water to the boil and cook the slices for 1–2 minutes.

4. Place green (spring) onions on a hot grill or under a broiler and cook for 1 minute on each side or until well marked.

5. Heat udonji until boiling. Pour 1 cup/8fl oz/250ml into each serving bowl. Top with sliced duck, spring onions, mitsuba sprigs, and soba balls.

Ingredients

4oz/120g soba noodle

4oz/120g duck breast, cut into 16 thin slices

1 tbsp/15g arrowroot

8 green (spring) onions, white stem only

4 cups/1¾ pints/1 litre udonji

4 sprigs mitsuba

Crispy Buckwheat Noodle Soup with Duck Breast (Age Soba and Kamo Shirumono)

Method

1. Combine saikyou miso, garlic, and mixed herbs in a large glass bowl. Place salmon in bowl. Spoon marinade over salmon. Refrigerate for 3 days, turning salmon daily.

2. Remove salmon from marinade and wipe dry with paper towel. Cook under a hot grill for 2–3 minutes each side, until deep golden in color.

3. Top salmon with crisp fried potato strips and deep fried salmon skin. Serve with cooked white and green asparagus.

Grilled Saikyou Miso Marinated Salmon with Herbs (Salmon Saikyou Yaki Kousou Huumi)

Ingredients

½ cup/4fl oz/125ml saikyou miso

1½ tsp/45g sliced garlic

2 tbsp/50g chopped mixed herbs eg rosemary, thyme, oregano

4x7oz/200g salmon cutlets, boneless

3oz/80g thin potato strips

1 sheet deep-fried salmon skin, cut into 4 strips

8 white asparagus spears, halved lengthwise

8 green asparagus spears, halved lengthwise

Method

1. Carefully open out the underside of the fish. With skin-side down, press the opening out flat with the palm of your hand. Gently remove the backbone, with tail still attached.

2. Straighten the shrimp by making cutlines along the underside and pushing backward.

3. Place the fish flesh, skin side down, on a board. Put the shrimp on top and wrap the fish around the shrimp. Place the fish on one edge of the nori and roll up.

4. Dust the nori roll with arrowroot and deep fry at 360°F/160°C for two minutes. Dust the fish spine with arrowroot and deep-fry until golden.

5. Place mixed seaweed on a serving plate. Cut nori parcel in half diagonally and arrange over seaweed. Arrange fried fish spine decoratively on plate. Garnish with steamed sugar snap peas, halved cherry tomatoes, and a lemon wedge. Spoon or pipe Ume sauce over sugar snap peas and serve.

Deep Fried Garfish Wrapped in Nori (Soyori Ebi Isobe-Age)

Ingredients

1 garfish or other white fish

1 large shrimp, peeled and deveined

½ sheet nori seaweed

arrowroot

¼oz/10g mixed seaweed

Ume sauce:

1 tsp/5ml Japanese plum sauce

1 tsp/5ml suiji

wasabi paste

47

Method

1. Lightly roll tofu cubes in arrowroot.

2. Deep fry tofu for 3–4 minutes.

3. Roll four cubes in seaweed powder to coat and four cubes in black sesame seeds.

4. Place one seaweed, one black sesame seed, and one plain tofu cube in each serving bowl.

5. Pour ⅓ cup/3½fl oz/100ml of udonji into each bowl.

Garnish with chives and serve.

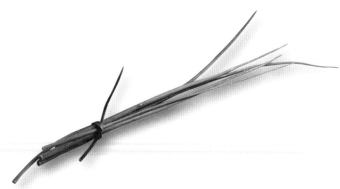

Three Kinds Deep-fried Tofu
(Sansyoku Agesuiji Tofu)

Ingredients

1 block (8oz/250g) tofu, cut into 12 squares

1 tsp/5g arrowroot

3 tsp/15g seaweed powder

3 tsp/15g black sesame seeds

1¾ cups/14fl oz/400ml udonji

2 tbsp/30g minced chives

Method

1. Fry all ingredients on a hot flat griddle, until just cooked.

2. Cut beef into thin slices and serve decoratively on a heated serving platter. Arrange cooked fish and vegetables on plate.

3. Serve with a bowl of onion sauce and garlic chips.

Onion sauce

1 Heat mirin and saké in a small saucepan until boiling. Remove from heat. Place all ingredients, including mirin and saké into the bowl of a food processor.

Process until smooth.

Make 2½ cups/1 pint/450ml

Ingredients

1 jumbo shrimp

4 slices calamari

2½ oz/60g slice porterhouse steak

½ cup/4oz/120g bean shoots

2 oyster mushrooms

2 slices red bell pepper

Onion Sauce

⅓ cup/3½fl oz/100ml mirin

2 tbsp/30ml sake

2 onions minced

⅓ cup/3½fl oz/100ml soy sauce

½ tsp/2.5g minced garlic

2 tbsp/30ml canola oil

2 slices leek

Assorted Seafood, Beef and Vegetables
Cooked on a Steel Plate (Kawara Yaki)

Method

1. To make batter, place flour, cornstarch, and chili powder in a bowl, mix to combine, and make a well in the center. Whisk in egg and water and beat until smooth. Add ice cubes

2. Heat oil in a deep saucepan until a cube of bread dropped in browns in 50 seconds.

3. Dip shrimp, snow peas, eggplant (aubergine) and broccoli florets in batter and deep-fry a few at a time for 3–4 minutes or until golden and crisp. Serve immediately.

4. See page 40 for Tempura batter

Serving suggestion: All that is needed to make this a complete meal is a variety of purchased dipping sauces, chutneys, relishes, and a tossed green salad.

Chili Tempura

Ingredients

vegetable oil for deep-frying

500g/1lb uncooked large shrimp, peeled and deveined, tails left intact

12 snow peas (mangetout), trimmed

1 eggplant (aubergine), cut into thin slices

1 small head broccoli, broken into small florets

Tempura Batter

85g/3oz self-rising flour

½ cup/60g/2oz cornstarch

1 teaspoon chili powder

1 egg, lightly beaten

1 cup/225ml/8fl oz iced water

4 ice cubes

Method

1. To make the dough, place parsley, egg white, and water into food processor and process for one minute. Sift the flour into a bowl and add parsley mixture. Knead together until smooth. Add rock salt and knead lightly for 1–2 minutes. Cover and allow to rest.

2. Remove abalone from shell and clean. Wash out shell. Place kelp sheet into the abalone shell and top with the abalone meat.

3. Arrange mushrooms, white radish, carrot, and yuzu peel over the abalone.

4. Roll out the dough to a ½in/1cm thickness and place over abalone shell, sealing top and any holes in shell.

5. Bake at 450°F/230°C for 20 minutes.

6. Serve with ponzu sauce.

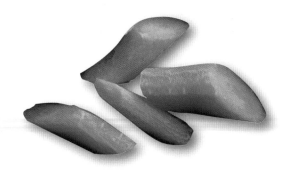

Abalone and Mushroom Baked in Salt Pastry (Awabiknoka Shiogamayaki)

Ingredients

Salt pastry, ½ cup/4oz/125g parsley

1 egg white, 2 tbsp/30ml water

3½oz/100g all-purpose flour, 30g rock salt

1 x 1lb/400g abalone

1 x 4in/10cm square kelp sheet, soaked

in water until soft

2 oyster mushrooms

1 shiitake mushroom

¼oz/10g enoki mushrooms

1 large decorative slice white radish

1 slice carrot

pinch yuzu peel

ponzu sauce

Method

1. Cut vegetables into¼–½in/5–10mm slices.

2. Dust vegetables lightly with flour.

3. Heat oil in deep fryer to 360°F/180°C.

4. Dip vegetables into tempura batter and deep fry until golden and crispy.

5. Drain lightly on kitchen paper and serve with tempura sauce.

Tempura Vegetables (Yasai Tempura)

Ingredients

3 slices lotus root

1 slice eggplant

1 small carrot, sliced in half lengthwise

2 asparagus

3 ginko nuts, threaded onto a bamboo skewer

5 spring onions, white parts only

3 slices sweet potato

2 slices zucchini

all-purpose flour

1¼ cups/10fl oz/300ml tempura batter

⅔ cup/5fl oz/150ml tempura sauce

Tip

Do not beat tempura batter until smooth, it needs

to be lumpy.

Method

1. Cook steak under a hot broiler for 1–2 minutes on each side (until very rare). Slice into very thin pieces.

2. Arrange beef on a platter, folding, and overlapping slightly.

3. Combine red onion, daikon, and moniji oroshi (to taste). Serve next to beef, with ponzu soy sauce, minced green (spring) onions, and lemon wedge.

Ingredients

3oz/80g porterhouse steak

¼ red onion, thinly sliced

1 tsp/5g grated daikon

1 tsp/5g moniji oroshi (chili paste)

1½ tbsp/20ml ponzu soy sauce

1 tbsp/15g minced green (spring) onion

wedge of lemon

Sliced Seared Beef with Ponzu Soy Sauce (Guy Tataki)

Method

1. Place the steaks in a non-metallic dish. Pour the teriyaki or soy sauce and olive oil over them and turn the steaks to coat. Cover and marinate for 1–2 hours in the refrigerator. Mix the crème fraîche and horseradish in a small bowl, then cover and refrigerate.

2. Heat a ridged cast-iron grill pan over medium-to-high heat. Brush with peanut oil, using a folded piece of kitchen towel. Alternatively, heat the oil in a heavy-based frying pan. Add 2 steaks, reserving the marinade, then cook for 3 minutes on each side, or until cooked to your liking. Remove and keep warm. Cook the remaining 2 steaks, then remove and keep warm.

3. Put the sliced green (spring) onions, garlic, chili peppers, and reserved marinade into a small saucepan and heat through. Spoon over the steaks and top with a dollop of the horseradish cream and shredded spring (green) onion. Serve the rest of the horseradish cream separately.

Japanese Beef with Horseradish Cream

Ingredients

4 rump steaks (170g/6oz each), trimmed of fat

4 tbsp/60ml teriyaki or soy sauce

4 tbsp/60ml olive oil

6 tbsp/90ml crème fraîche

4 tsp/20ml creamed horseradish

2 tsp/10ml groundnut oil

7 spring (green) onions, thinly sliced,

1 spring (green) onion

2 garlic cloves, chopped

¼ tsp/1.25g dried crushed chili peppers

Method

Combine the lime juice with the rice wine and crushed garlic. Marinate the bay scallops for 15 minutes. Set aside.

While the scallops are marinating, grate the ginger, slice the spring (green) onions, and mushrooms, and dice the red bell pepper. Heat the sesame oil in a hot wok or large skillet until almost smoking.

To the wok, add the ginger, spring (green) onions, mushrooms, and red bell pepper. Stir-fry for about 3 minutes, until the ginger has become fragrant. Add the scallops and marinade. Continue stir-frying for another 3 minutes, until scallops have become opaque, mixing the wok ingredients together well. Add the soy sauce; mix thoroughly. Pepper to taste.

Dilute the cornstarch with water and pour the liquid into the wok. Cook for another minute or two or until the sauce has thickened and become smooth.

Serve immediately with steamed white rice.

Ginger Scallop Stir-Fry

Ingredients

2 tbsp/30ml fresh lime juice

2 tbsp/30ml rice wine

1 garlic clove, crushed

8oz/250g scallops

1 tbsp/15ml sesame oil

2 tsp/10ml ginger, finely grated

4 spring (green) onions, cut diagonally into ½-inch lengths

½ red bell pepper, diced

3oz/75g button mushrooms, sliced

2 tsp/10ml soy sauce

pinch of black pepper, 1 tsp/5g cornstarch

2 tbsp/30ml water

Method

1. Peel skin from tongue. Heat oil in frying pan and cook tongue until well browned all over.

2. Place tongue, red wine, mirin, and water into pressure cooker. Seal and cook for 2½ hours.

3. Remove tongue from cooking liquid, cover, and keep warm.

4. Bring cooking liquid to the boil and reduce for 10 minutes.

5. Slice tongue and arrange on serving plates.

6. Drizzle sweet miso sauce over the sliced tongue. Garnish with shredded leek, white sesame seeds, and parsley sprigs.

Ingredients

1 tbsp/15ml canola oil

1 whole ox tongue

1½ cups/12fl oz/350ml red wine

½ cup/4fl oz/125ml mirin

1 cup/8fl oz/250ml water

¼ cup/2fl oz/50ml sweet miso sauce

Braised Ox Tongue with Miso Sauce and Red Wine (Gyutan Akawainni Amamisozoe)

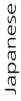

shredded leek

white sesame seeds

parsley sprigs

Japanese

Method

1. Place the chicken in a glass bowl, mix marinade ingredients together. and pour over chicken. Cover and place in refrigerator to marinate for several hours or overnight.

2. Thread 2 tenderloins onto each skewer, using a weaving motion. Heat barbecue or electric grill to medium-high. Grease grill bars or griddle lightly with oil.

3. Place skewers in a row, and cook for 2 minutes on each side, brushing with marinade as they cook, and when turned. Remove to a large serving platter. Serve immediately as finger food.

Ingredients

1lb/500g chicken breasts

Marinade

¼ cup/60ml/2fl oz teriyaki sauce

¼ cup/60ml/2fl oz honey

1 garlic clove, crushed

¼ tsp/1.25g ginger, ground

small bamboo skewers, soaked

oil for greasing

Chicken Yakitori

Japanese

Method

1. Cut each quail in half and remove the backbones and ribs from the meat.

2. Combine all marinade ingredients. Place quail halves in a flat glass dish. Pour marinade over them. Allow to marinate for 12–24 hours.

3. Make a few slashes, ½in/1cm apart, 1in/2cm in length, in each wonton sheet. Deep-fry each sheet, one at a time, so that it opens out like a fan. Remove when golden.

4. Heat butter in a frying pan, add garlic and mushrooms, and pan-fry for 2–3 minutes until mushrooms are tender and golden. Remove from heat, stir in shallots and chives.

5. Cook quail on a hot grill or under a hot broiler for 3 minutes each side, until well browned.

6. Spoon mushrooms onto a heated serving platter, top with the wonton fan. Arrange quail on top. Garnish with shredded leek and serve.

Grilled Quail

Ingredients

4 quail	2 tsp/10g butter
Marinade:	2 tsp/10g minced garlic
⅔ cup/5fl oz/150ml red wine	4 oyster mushrooms
⅓ cup/3½fl oz/100ml mirin	4 shiitake mushrooms
½ cup/4fl oz/125ml soy sauce	3 tbsp/1½ oz/40g enoki mushrooms
1 tsp/5g crushed black pepper	2 shallots, minced
4 bayleaves	1 tbsp/15g minced chives
4 wonton sheets	salt, ¼ cup julienned leek

Method:

1. Carefully slice eel lengthwise through the center, to create two very thin fillets. Then cut each piece in half. Sprinkle with mountain pepper.

2. Cook wonton dough in boiling water for 2–3 minutes, until tender. Drain.

3. Arrange two sheets of cooked wonton dough over the base of a 10cm x 20cm/4x8in rectangular container.

4. Arrange half the mixture lettuce leaves on top of pastry. Place half the eel over the lettuce. Top with another layer of wonton pastry. Cover with remaining lettuce, eel and wonton pastry. Gently press down.

5. Squeeze out any moisture from the mushrooms and chop finely. Combine mushrooms, ponzu, and olive oil. Cut lasagne into four and serve with mushroom sauce.

Ingredients

1 grilled eel (Unagi No Kobayaki), around 200g/7oz

pinch of Japanese mountain pepper (sansho)

6 sheets wonton dough

2oz/50g mixed salad leaves

Cold Served Grilled Eel Lasagne
(Una Gi Wanton Salad)

4 dried shiitake mushrooms, soaked in water for 2-3 hours

⅓ cup ponzu soy sauce

2 tablespoons extra virgin olive oil

Japanese

Method

1. Arrange sliced beef decoratively on a plate. Place all vegetables and tofu on another platter.

2. Heat beef fat in a sukiyaki pan (or other heavy-based frying pan) on the serving table. Cook some of each ingredient while adding a little sukiyaki sauce to the pan. Cook for only a few minutes before serving. Guests may choose to dip the cooked ingredients into the beaten egg before eating.

3. Continue to cook remaining ingredients while adding a little more sukiyaki sauce to the pan as required.

To make Sukyaki Sauce: Place all ingredients in a saucepan and heat until sugar has dissolved.

Sukiyaki

Ingredients

4oz/120g marbled porterhouse steak

3½oz/100g Chinese cabbage

½ onion, sliced

2 shiitake mushrooms

4 pieces sliced carrot, 8 cubes tofu

4 spring (green) onions

50g syungiku, 1oz/30g beef fat

2 eggs, beaten

Sukiyaki Sauce

1¼ cups/10fl oz/300ml mirin

1¼ cups/10fl oz/300ml soy sauce

½ cup/4fl oz/130ml saké,

½ cup/4oz/130g sugar

⅓ cup/3½fl oz/100ml suiji

Method

1. Place chicken under a hot broiler and cook for two minutes each side. Heat teriyaki sauce in a large frying pan. Place chicken into pan and cook for a further two minutes on each side. Slice each chicken fillet into ½in/1cm strips. Arrange carefully onto warmed serving plate.

2. Combine vegetables with sugar, light soy sauce, and sesame oil. Stir fry over a high heat for 1–2 minutes.

3. Arrange vegetables beside the chicken, sprinkle with sesame seeds and serve.

Teriyaki sauce

Combine all ingredients in a saucepan. Heat until sugar has dissolved. Remove from heat and allow to cool.

Makes 3¾ cups/1½ pints/850ml

Teriyaki Chicken with Kinpira Vegetables (Teriyaki Wakadori Teriyaki, Kinpira)

Ingredients

4 chicken breast fillets

1 cup/8fl oz/250ml teriyaki sauce

4 green asparagus, cut into quarters

4 white asparagus, cut into quarters

4 baby carrots, cut into quarters lengthwise

4 baby corn, cut into quarters lengthwise

1 tbsp/15g sugar

1 tbsp/15ml light soy sauce

2 tsp/10ml sesame oil

2 tsp/10g white sesame seeds

Teriyaki Sauce

1¾ cups/14fl oz/400ml mirin

1½ cups/12fl oz/350ml soy sauce

3½fl oz/100ml saké

⅓ cup/3oz/80g sugar

Method

1. Place suiji into a medium saucepan, bring to the boil. Add daikon, reduce heat, and allow to simmer for about 20 minutes or until tender.

2. Place duck fillets, skin-side down, in a medium hot frying pan. Cook for 4–5 minutes on each side, until medium rare. Cut each fillet into thin slices. Place a piece of cooked daikon on each serving plate and top with duck slices. Spoon sauce over duck and place fried lotus root slices on top.

3. Serve with cooked snow peas and grilled leek.

Ingredients

3 cups/1¼ pints/750ml suiji

1 medium daikon, peeled and cut into quarters lengthwise

4 duck breast fillets

20 slices lotus root, deep fried until golden

¼ cup/2oz/50g snow peas

1 leek, cut into julienne strips

⅓ cup/3½fl oz/100ml jaone sauce

Duck Breast Fillet Teriyaki
with Japanese Mountain Pepper
(Kamo Teriyaki Arimazahsyo Huumi)

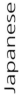

Japanese

Method

1. Cook turnip in boiling water until tender, then drain. Cook scallops in boiling water for 5 seconds, drain and cool in refrigerator. Combine turnip, scallops, paw paw and chives.

2. Combine all miso dressing ingredients, add scallop mixture and stir well. Spoon half of the mixture onto the center of each serving dish.

3. Cut daikon into ¼in/5mm strips. Cut three strips to measure 1inx8in/3cm by 20cm. Wrap a strip around the scallop mixture. Secure by tying a chive around the outside. Lightly press down the scallop mixture to form a flat surface.

4. Spoon tobiko and caviar decoratively over the top. Garnish with chives and serve.

Brunoise Scallop Salad Aya Style (Hotate Kabu Reisei)

Ingredients

4oz/120g turnip, cut into 5mm dice

8 scallops, cut into ¼in/5 mm dice

3oz/80g papaya, cut into 5mm dice

½ cup/4oz/125g chopped chives

Miso dressing:

1 tbsp/15ml saké

1 tbsp/15ml mirin

1 tbsp/15ml light soy sauce

1 tbsp/15ml rice vinegar

2 tsp/10g ponzu

4fl oz/120g saikyou miso

1 tbsp/15g minced onion

1 tbsp/15ml extra virgin olive oil

2 tsp/10ml wholegrain mustard

1 tsp/5ml ginger juice

1 large cooked daikon, ⅓ cup/3½oz/100g tobiko

⅓ cup caviar, chives

Method

1. Deep-fry eggplant and zucchini for 4 minutes, drain on kitchen paper. Steam or boil remaining vegetables until tender. Arrange decoratively on a large platter.

2. Top each vegetable with a tablespoon of a different flavored miso.

For example:

Eggplant topped with torimiso and broiled

until golden brown

Zucchini topped with black miso

Carrots topped with walnut miso

Turnip topped with white miso

Japanese taro topped with yuzumiso

Yellow squash topped with syungiku miso

Miso Sauces (for Dengaku)

1 Combine all ingredients in a saucepan. Heat until sugar has dissolved. Remove from heat and allow to cool.

Makes 3¾ cups/1½ pints/850ml

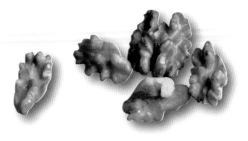

Assorted Dengaku (Dengaku Iroiro)

Ingredients

½ baby eggplant, ½ small zucchini

2 baby carrots, 1 baby turnip

5 Japanese taro, 1 yellow squash

Miso Sauces (for Dengaku)

1¾ cups/14fl oz/400ml mirin,

1½ cups/12fl oz/350ml soy sauce

⅓ cup/3½fl oz/100ml saké

2½ tbsp/2½oz/80g sugar

White Miso

2 tsp/10ml mirin, 1 tbsp/15ml saké

2½ oz/70g sugar, 3½ oz/100g saikyou miso

Black Miso

1 tbsp/15ml mirin, 1 tbsp/15ml saké

⅓ cup/3oz/90g sugar, 100g dark miso

Method

Soak agar agar in water until soft, around 30 minutes. Squeeze out excess water and tear into pieces

Combine ingredients for sobatsuyu in a saucepan. Heat and allow to simmer. Add half the agar agar and stir until it has dissolved. Divide sobatsuyu evenly between three rectangular containers measuring 3inx12in/8cm by 30cm each. Refrigerate until set.

Heat suiji in a saucepan until simmering. Add remaining agar agar and stir until it has dissolved. Remove from heat.

Evenly cover surface of each sobatsuyu jelly with one type of noodle. Pour a little suiji over each of the noodles.

Top the green tea noodles with some chicken and carrot. Pour over more suiji to cover.

Cover the shiso noodles with mashed egg yolk and sliced okra. Cover with suiji.

Cut shrimp in half, lengthwise. Arrange shrimp and beans over sumen noodles. Pour over suiji to cover.

Refrigerate all three jellies until set. Carefully remove from molds. Slice each jelly into four pieces, each measuring approximately 3inx2in/8cmx5cm.

Arrange three different jellies on each serving dish.

Ingredients

3 sticks Japanese agar agar

Sobatsuyu:

3¾ cups/900ml fish broth

⅓ cup/3½fl oz/100ml mirin

⅓ cup/3½fl oz/100ml mirin

4 cups/1¾ pints/1 litre suiji

2oz/50g green tea noodles, cooked

2oz/50g shisa noodles, cooked

A Trio of Noodle Agar Agar Jellies
(Sansyoku Soba Yosemono)

2oz/50g sumen noodles, cooked

1¾oz/40g cooked chicken breast, shredded

1 small carrot, sliced thinly

1 cooked egg yolk, lightly mashed

1 cooked okra, sliced thinly

4 small cooked shrimp, peeled and deveined

2 green beans, cut into 1 in/2cm lengths

Japanese

Method

1. Stir together marscapone and Tia Maria. Separate eggs and beat egg yolks and castor sugar until light and fluffy.

2. Beat egg whites until soft peaks form. Gently fold in marscapone mixture and beaten egg yolks.

3. Place green tea, sambucca, sugar, and water in a small saucepan and stir over a medium heat until sugar has dissolved.

4. Place a layer of sponge in an 8inx8in/20cm x 20cm square dish. Pour half the syrup over it. Spread with half the marscapone mixture. Top with the remaining sponge, syrup and marscapone mixture. Refrigerate for four hours or overnight if possible.

5. Carefully cut into eight triangles. Serve with a sprinkle of green tea powder and some fresh berries.

Green Tea Tiramisù Flavored with Sambucca (Macha Sambucca Tiramisu)

Ingredients

7oz/200g marscapone

1½ tbsp/20ml Tia Maria

2 eggs

1½ tbsp/20g superfine (castor) sugar

1½ tbsp/20g green tea powder

2 tbsp/30ml sambucca

1½ tbsp/20g sugar

5 tbsp/70ml water

2 x 8inx8in (20cm x 20cm) pieces sponge cake

Method

1. Place fish, arrowroot, saké, mirin, light soy sauce, sugar, egg white, and salt into the bowl of a food processor. Process to a smooth paste.

2. Spoon paste into a bowl and combine with crab, onion, green (spring) onions and ginger.

3. Whisk egg yolk with a few drops of canola oil. Continue to add oil, a drop at a time, while whisking to form a mayonnaise-style dressing. Add to crab mixture and stir well.

4. Cut each wonton sheet in half and then slice into very thin strips, 1⁄16in/1–2mm wide.

5. Take a heaping tablespoon of crab mixture and carefully form into a ball. Press wonton strips over the ball to coat it. Repeat with remaining crab mixture and wonton dough to create 12 balls. Press a crab claw into the top of each of the dumpling balls.

6. Steam dumplings for 10 minutes.

Serve with ponzu soy sauce.

Ingredients

7oz/200g fish fillet, such as snapper

2 tbsp/30g arrowroot

1 tbsp/15ml cooking saké

1 tbsp/15ml mirin

1 tbsp/15ml light soy sauce

1 tsp/5g sugar

1 egg white

salt, to taste

7oz/200g steamed crabmeat, shredded

½ onion, minced

4 spring (green) onions, chopped

2 tsp/10g grated ginger

1 egg yolk

Steamed Crab Dumplings
(Kani Mushimono)

½ cup canola oil

15 wonton sheets

12 small crab claws

ponzu soy sauce

Method

1. Place milk, cream, and sugar in a saucepan. Heat gently until sugar has dissolved. Remove from heat. Carefully sprinkle gelatin over the mixture and stir until dissolved. Stir in amaretto.

2. Divide mixture into three equal parts.

Stir black sesame paste into one third.

Mix white sesame paste into another third, and leave the last plain.

3. Pour the black sesame blancmange into the base of four cold dessert glasses. Carefully pour the white sesame blancmange over this. Finally top with the plain blancmange. Refrigerate 1–2 hours until set.

4. Top each blancmange with 1 tbsp/15ml kuromitsu sauce and some broken caramelised filo. Serve with some mixed berries.

To make:

Caramelised Filo. Place one sheet filo dough on a greased cookie sheet, sprinkle with lightly with some sugar. Place under a hot broiler until sugar caramelizes. Remove from heat and immediately sprinkle with white sesame seeds. Allow to cool. Break into pieces.

Black Sesame Blancmange
(Kuro Gomo Blanc Manger)

Ingredients

1 scant cup/7fl oz/200ml milk

1¼ cups10fl oz/300ml thickened cream

2½ tbsp/45g sugar

1 tbsp/15g powdered unflavored gelatin

3 tsp/15ml amaretto

2 tbsp/30ml black sesame paste

2 tbsp/30ml white sesame paste

4 tbsp/60ml kuromitsu sauce

1 sheet caramelized filo

Method

1. Lay 1 piece of filo dough on a board. Place a whole banana near one corner. Spoon 2 tbsp/30ml red bean paste and ½ tsp/2.5g yuzu peel beside the banana. Roll up dough to fully enclose banana, like a parcel.

2. Heat oil to 360°F/180°C and deep fry banana parcel for 3–4 minutes, until golden.

3. Repeat with remaining ingredients.

4. Cut banana in half diagonally, dust with confectioner's sugar and serve each with 1 tbsp/15ml kuromitsu.

Ingredients

4 sheets filo dough

4 bananas, peeled

½ cup/4oz/125ml red bean paste

2 tsp/10g yuzu peel

confectioner's (icing) sugar

4 tbsp/60ml kuromitsu

Deep Fried Banana Wrapped
in Filo (Banana Tsutsumi Age)

Method

1. Place milk, egg yolks, sugar, and arrowroot into the top of a double boiler. Stir over boiling water until custard thickens and coats the back of a wooden spoon. Remove from heat and allow to cool.

2. Stir in Cointreau, mashed pumpkin, and yuzu peel.

3. Place ingredients into an ice cream-maker and churn until frozen.

Purple Congo Ice Cream (Murasaki Imo Ice)

1. Place milk, egg yolks, sugar, and arrowroot into the top of a double-boiler. Stir over boiling water until custard thickens and coats the back of a wooden spoon. Remove from heat and allow to cool.

2. Stir in Malibu, purple congo, and sweet potato.

3. Place ingredients into an icecream maker and churn until frozen.

Assorted Ice Cream Black Sesame Ice Cream (Kuro Goma Ice)

1. Place milk, cream, egg yolks and sugar into the top of a double boiler. Stir over boiling water until custard thickens and coats the back of a wooden spoon. Remove from heat and allow to cool.

2. Stir in black sesame paste.

3. Place ingredients into an icecream maker and churn until frozen.

Assorted Ice Cream Pumpkin and Yuzu Ice Cream (Kabocha and Yuzu Ice)

Ingredients

1¾ cups/14fl oz/400ml milk

4 egg yolks, lightly beaten

½ cup/4oz/120g sugar, 1 tbsp arrowroot

2 tsp/10ml Cointreau

Pumpkin Ice Cream

1¾ cups/14fl oz400g pumpkin, cooked and mashed

1 tbsp/15g chopped yuzu peel

Purple Congo Ice Cream (Murasaki Imo Ice)

14fl oz/400ml milk, 4 eggs yolks, lightly beaten

½ cup/4oz/120g sugar, 1 tbsp/15g arrowroot

1 tbsp/15ml Malibu liqueur

4oz/120g purple congo potato, steamed and mashed

10oz/280g sweet potato, steamed and mashed

Black Sesame Ice Cream (Kuro Goma Ice)

1¾ cups/14fl oz/400ml milk

1 scant cup/7fl oz/200ml cream

4 egg yolks, 3 tbsp/80g sugar

½ cup/4oz/125g black sesame paste

Method

1. Combine egg yolks, cream, milk, and sugar. Mix until smooth. Divide mixture into two equal halves.

2. Add green tea powder and sambucca to one of the mixtures. Stir well. Add yuzu peel and Cointreau to the second mixture.Mix well.

3. Pour each mixture into four greased 1 cup/8oz/250g ramekins. Place ramekins into a bain-marie where warm water comes ⅓ of the side up the ramekins.

4. Bake at 360°/180°C for 20 minutes.

5. Remove from bain marie and allow to cool. Refrigerate for at least 2 hours. Carefully turn out one of each brulée onto each serving place.

6. Sprinkle 1 tsp/5g sugar over each brulée. Place under a hot broiler for 2–3 minutes until sugar has caramelized.

Yuzu and Green Tea Brulée

Ingredients

4 egg yolks	1 tbsp/15g green tea (gunpowder)
1 scant cup/7fl oz/200ml heavy cream	2 tsp/10ml sambucca
5½fl oz/160ml milk	½ tsp/2.5g yuzu peel
⅓ cup/3½oz/100g superfine (castor) sugar	2 tsp/10ml Cointreau

Index